FREEDOM FROM
FEAR

HOW TO LIVE IN VICTORY IN A TIME OF CRISIS

FREEDOM FROM
FEAR

HOW TO LIVE IN VICTORY IN A TIME OF CRISIS

EMMA STARK

Dedication

To my Glasgow Prophetic Centre family, who have held the truth of freedom and deliverance as a core value and have applied their authority so rigorously that many now walk in liberty.

DESTINY IMAGE® PUBLISHERS, INC.

P.O. Box 310, Shippensburg, PA 17257-0310

"Promoting Inspired Lives."

This book and all other Destiny Image and Destiny Image Fiction books are available at Christian bookstores and distributors worldwide.

Cover design by: Eileen Rockwell

For more information on foreign distributors, call 717-532-3040.

Reach us on the Internet: www.destinyimage.com.

ISBN 13 TP: 978-0-7684-5679-0

ISBN 13 eBook: 978-0-7684-5667-7

For Worldwide Distribution.

1 2 3 4 5 6 7 8 / 24 23 22 21 20

Contents

Introduction

Shaking: Our New Normal

This is what the Lord Almighty says: "In a little while I will once more shake the heavens and the earth, the sea and the dry land. I will shake all nations, and what is desired by all nations will come, and I will fill this house with glory," says the Lord Almighty. "The silver is mine and the gold is mine," declares the Lord Almighty. "The glory of this present house will be greater than the glory of the former house," says the Lord Almighty. "And in this place I will grant peace," declares the Lord Almighty (Haggai 2:6-9).

We live in a turbulent time. Emotionally, it feels bumpy and choppy, and it could be very easy to become overwhelmed by it all. It's as if we're standing with shifting tectonic plates under our feet and we're fighting to find our balance and our equilibrium. Nothing is familiar; nothing is the same.

We are in a pivot—or hinge—moment in the story of the earth that Jesus is writing. Forevermore, historians will speak of this time as the "reset" time—the moment of earthly recalibration, the time the world shifted and changed.

"Coronavirus!" and threat of the disease it causes (COVID-19) is screamed from every news media outlet with a constant, unrelenting force, as the cold fingers of fear try to wrap themselves around our planet. Theories, counter-theories, and conspiracies abound and millions of voices clamor for our attention. And, all the while, our all-pervasive, all-consuming social media brings little to calm us. We've never been more connected—but at the same time we've never been so socially distant from one another.

And yet, throughout it all, the Lord God Almighty is still seated on His throne. His seat of government is not a distant, far-off monarchy but is a consistent, ever-present, close-at-hand reality.

So, what is our God up to? What is His plan? And how do we live in this new dynamic, where the storms of change have become the new "normal"?

> **How do we live when the storms of change have become the new "normal"?**

God Is Investing in Shaking

God is *investing* in shaking the earth and the heavens so that another level of glory may come to us. But let's be clear—this is *not* God in angry mode. This is *not* God in judgement mode either. This is God in glory-sharing mode.

God is never caught off guard like we are. Nor is He surprised when things happen to us. He always works with a plan; He always has a divine order. According to the verses from Haggai 2 that I quoted above, in God's cycles *shaking comes first*.

In the early stages of shaking, everything that is not built by God gets shaken and nothing is left out. Structures, attitudes, churches, places, families, governments, homes, locations, beliefs and prejudices, jobs, friendships—all get the "investment" of God's hand, shaking and challenging them to their core.

This is the kindness of God to the earth, because there is very little effective preaching without shaking, very little growth without challenge, very little revival without crisis, very little change without agitation. Look back in your life and think about those times when you really changed for the better, learned something new, or saw a miracle—was it in the comfortable times or in the testing times that you experienced breakthrough?

Shaking gets your attention and a crisis drives men to seek God. Can we be real with each other here? We would all love to learn in the midst of times of blessing and stability and to seek God during the abundances of our life, but we—and the rest of humanity—rarely behave in that way. We require tumultuousness and upheaval to change. Shaking provokes the church to witness to the world. Shaking drives us from our pettiness and our idolatries.

**Shaking provokes the church to
witness to the world.**

After the shaking, the glory comes. The shaking expands and increases our capacity to steward increased glory and harvest.

We are at the beginning of an epic decade, where the destination point is the *glory of the Lord covering the earth* (see Hab. 2:14) with mass salvations and demonstrations of Kingdom power like we have never seen before—through the hands of the church.

We are walking into a move of the Holy Spirit and all He does will be seen. Remember, the Holy Spirit is for *all* the church and for *all* the world. He is not supposed to be locked up inside churches or to be seen only by a few Charismatic or Pentecostal types of churchgoer. No! He is on the move—and a full wave of the glory of God is about to crash over us!

It is because of this global shaking hitting us now that there will then be an outpouring of the Holy Spirit that ignites a global revival.

Therefore, embrace the fact that God is challenging you deeply and that you do not have all the answers right now. Lean in, with joy, to your uncomfortableness.

Welcome the reality that God is shaking you and everything around about you. With an adventuring attitude, receive the turbulence that is God's gift to you. *Choose your attitude in the shaking.* Do not resist the shaking. Instead, it is time to pray that you would be shaken—according to God's plan—so that you might be a renewed version of yourself with everything that needs to be stripped away and readjusted now accomplished in you. We are *not* in the days when we only cry out, "Show me Your glory!" Instead, we cry out to be shaken—so that we might then *carry His glory* in an increased way. In other words: if you feel challenged and shaken, then you are right on time with the season of God.

> **Cry out to be shaken—so that you might then carry His glory in an increased way.**

A Vision: God Travailing on His Knees

Recently I had a shocking open vision in which I saw Father God. He stood up from His throne and got down on His hands and knees to travail and cry over the earth. Initially I was uncertain about how to respond to such a sight, but I was beckoned by the angelic host to come closer and to join in with what God was doing as a co-laborer. So I knelt down, mirroring God's position. Many Scriptures coursed through my mind, especially the images of Jesus weeping over Jerusalem (see Luke 19) and the truth of God acting like a laboring woman, as described by Isaiah:

> *I have kept silent for a long time, I have kept still and restrained Myself. Now like a woman in labor I will groan, I will both gasp and pant* (Isaiah 42:14 NASB).

We are perhaps more comfortable with images of God arising as a mighty man of war or happier to dwell on pictures of Jesus as a kindly shepherd. But the very idea of God on His hands and knees, laboring uncomfortably, announces to us that all things are passing away and that He is indeed bringing about something new. Consider it! Father God, with groans and deep sighs, panting with effort and crying out, face contorted, tears plentiful, and, perhaps like His Son in Gethsemane, with bloodied sweat on His brow.

Is this what God feels like when He sees our daily dishonesty and idolatries?

Is this what God does when he sees our routine un-kindnesses?

Is this God's response when He measures our fear and finds us paralyzed into inaction by it?

Is this Isaiah 42 pose regularly frequented by God?

I crept in beside Him and heard an intensity in His utterances. He was crying over the nations, calling with urgency for them to choose Him. "Choose Me while I can be found! Choose Me, nations! I *will* have My inheritance!" He was calling for people to find Him as He shook the earth.

God had waved His hand across the earth, enabling great challenges so that He could be found. It is from this vantage point that we must look at what is going on all around us. We must look through *His* window on the eternal perspective rather than down the narrow line of sight that we currently peer through. Our tiny, myopic gaze means that we are continually consumed by what is right in front of us, as if this present day, right here, right now is all that matters. But God sees eternity—and does what is necessary to help secure a place for us with Him in it.

> **God does what is necessary to help secure a place for us with Him in eternity.**

Shakings and Catastrophes in Scripture

Shaking and catastrophes are well explained to us in Scripture and they should not come as a shock to us. We do not need to be prophets to foretell times that will trouble the earth—we simply need to read the Bible!

> *You will hear of wars and rumors of wars, but see to it that you are not alarmed. Such things must happen, but the end is still to come. Nation will rise against nation, and kingdom against kingdom. There will be famines and earthquakes in various places. All these are the beginning of birth pains* (Matthew 24:6-8).

Perhaps the key truth from these verses is not that negative and alarming things will happen but that we are expected to not be alarmed. The biblical refrain of "*do not be alarmed*" should fill our minds. "Do not be alarmed" must be truth that repetitively washes over us. "Do not be alarmed" needs to be the medicine we imbibe and must be the "pep-talk" to our emotions.

Let's Go on a Practical Journey Together

So, in this short book I invite you to come with me on a journey where we will get practical together. We'll work with specific prayers and decrees to realign your inner world so that it is not alarmed. Let's explore both the power of God *and* the freedom He has to give to you. Together we'll gain an understanding of how we deal with the demons of fear that lurk around us.

You're Going to Get Radically Free!

This book is action-packed, with a bespoke focus on personal deliverance from the demonic strongholds of fear and grief. If you are in bondage then take heart—in a few short pages you will be radically free!

Activation Prayer

It's time to speak this out loud over your life:

Heavenly Father, I praise You and thank You that You are on the throne and that You have a plan for the earth. I cry out to You that You would invest in the necessary shaking that my life needs.

I ask that You do this so that I might be more in Your image and made ready to steward greater glory. Shake out of me all that I need to lose. I repent of putting my faith in things other than You. Take away my idolatries and forgive my sins.

I speak over my own heart the words of Christ Jesus, "Do not be alarmed," and I say to You, God, "I trust You fully to look after me. Thank You that You have never let me down before and that I am on a sure footing with You."

In Jesus's name, amen!

Chapter 1

Jesus: The Supreme Power!

The Works of the Devil Are Destroyed

In order to lay hold of the spectacular freedom from fear that Jesus has to offer us, we must understand His mighty power and the smallness of our foe. We generally approach God and understand Him along familiar, well-trodden paths. Our prayers tend to be repetitive and lack a width and breadth of the fullness of who God is.

It is time to ask, "How freshly am I seeing God?" God is more than you have seen to date.

If I only see him as "Father," I will not know what it is to meet Him as the Isaiah 4 *Spirit of Burning.*

If I only see Him as friend, I will not know what it is to meet His justice.

If I only see Him as serious, I will not meet His laughter or His playfulness.

If I only see Him as the Ezekiel 1 God who sits on a throne, outside the circle of the Earth, I will not meet Him as the Isaiah 49 God as a nursing mother, suckling and weaning nations at His breast, shockingly intimate and deeply challenging.

There is a need to cry out for fresh eyes so that we might meet the vast expansiveness of God and be challenged by who He is—that His truth and His reality might meet our staleness and propel us into new life. Cry out so we might not "think" that we know Him— and repeat my stunted version of truth to others—when there is still a fresh ocean of who He is to be dived into!

> *For this purpose the Son of God was manifested, that He might destroy the works of the devil* (1 John 3:8 NKJV).

Satan (the devil) fears Jesus. Satan fears Jesus's methods; satan fears Jesus's will; satan fears Jesus's ways.

Satan fears the power that Jesus has placed in His church; satan fears Christians!

Have you ever thought about the three days that Jesus spent as a disembodied spirit after His death, before He burst out of the grave with resurrection life? After Jesus's crucified body was laid in the tomb, He had three days before He rose again. How did He spend that time? What did He do, who did He see, and where did He go?

Let's pull back the veil of what Scripture says and we'll see just how remarkable those world-changing seventy-two hours were. Immediately after His death, Jesus travelled down to the realm of the dead, to the departed spirits. He went to *Sheol* (also known as *Hades*), the city of the dead, where the grave held its prisoners. His successful strategy was to capture the keys of death and the grave, completely stripping away their power forevermore!

In *Sheol*, Jesus liberated all those who had been held there, including, no doubt, Abraham, Isaac, Jacob, David, John the Baptist, and the rest of the Bible's departed faithful. All those who had died and were considered righteous were ransomed from the power of the grave. Paul describes that Jesus gloriously, *"ascended on high, [leading] captive a host of captives"* (Eph. 4:8 NASB). He rose and took these people who had once been captives up in His train, breaking them out of the grave!

I don't imagine that Jesus snuck quietly into *Sheol*, ducking and diving like an undercover spy! Nor do I think he crept in on tiptoes, hiding behind the archangel Michael and hoping for a quick rescue while the guards' backs were turned! And I really don't believe that Jesus was poring over a map of *Sheol* for hours beforehand with the angel armies, constructing a stealth plan and a multi-pronged approach—just in case one of them was caught off-guard. On the contrary! This was the moment of the utter *terrorizing* of darkness! This was the very moment that all of Heaven had longed for, the very moment that satan had feared the most. And it happened moments after Jesus breathed His last breath, just when satan thought that he had won.

This was the moment of the utter terrorizing of darkness!

I imagine that at that instant every principality and power, whether for good or evil, had turned to Jerusalem to watch in the spirit-realm to see what Jesus's spirit would do after it left His crucified body. Surely this moment could not have been anything other than truly glorious—when Jesus strode right up to the very door of darkness, eyes blazing like fire and burning up all that was evil. If hills melt like wax before Him (see Ps. 97:5), would not death melt before Him also? No demon could possibly stand up; nothing evil could move—everyone and everything was frozen in awe. Jesus walked right up to the devil's most prized wall, the wall where satan hung his keys of death and the grave. He reached out his hand and, without hindrance or opposition, He roared, "MINE!" and took the keys back. Then, with every demon pinned to the ground because of the holiness that emanates from Him, Jesus began to preach! In these halls of darkness, the very home of depravity itself, Jesus stood and proclaimed to the spirits who were imprisoned there (see 1 Pet. 3:19). He was not scared in the slightest, nor did

He need to rush away. He lingered in *Sheol* to speak truth. Was it in this second that every demon suddenly understood the masterplan of salvation that had just unfolded in front of them? Was it in this flash of light that it dawned on satan that he had utterly failed?

Jesus must have walked out of that place just as He walked in—totally unscathed and accompanied by the liberated captives marching with Him. There is nothing that satan can do to stop Him, even on his own doorstep. Satan has to hear the preaching, has to watch people choose Jesus, and has to see his prisoners loosed right in the place he thought he had the ruler's position. It's no wonder that the Bible says, *"And having disarmed the powers and authorities, he made a public spectacle of them, triumphing over them by the cross"* (Col. 2:15). Jesus stripped away all of satan's trump cards. He completely decimated all that satan thought he was building, and, in that act, satan lost any real way to hold us prisoner.

In that act, satan lost any real way to hold us prisoner.

Stop Being Impressed with Satan and His Schemes

I pray that you would be able to see these seventy-two hours play out for yourself and that you would grasp hold of the need to *stop* being impressed or overwhelmed with anything that darkness brings against you. When you are standing in front of a need, or a great onslaught of darkness, or you are requiring a miracle, Jesus steps right into the heart of what looks like a stronghold of satan and He floods the situation with His power—the power that robs the enemy and destroys the plans of the evil one.

The devil is a withering branch! He has been cut off from the source of life and he is in decay. End your partnership with being impressed with him. Call time on allowing him to invade your world. You can destroy satan's power with Jesus—who is inside you—over and over again.

When time comes to an end and satan is finally bound, he is not even worthy of God's attention! One angel is sent forward to throw satan into the Abyss.

Satan is so small to the host of heaven and in comparison to the power of God that only one angel is required to remove him to await his eventual punishment (see Rev. 20:1-3,10).

There is more power in you, because of Jesus, than all of the strength of darkness combined. I bless you to step into a new powerful place and I release to you victory, to slay and trample on the darkness that surrounds you, just like your Savior modeled.

Activation Prayer

This is best spoken out loud:

> *Dear Jesus,*
>
> *Please help me to live unimpressed by satan.*
>
> *Help me to live in response to Father God only.*
>
> *Help me magnify You until You are so large that You fill my gaze completely.*
>
> *In Jesus's name, amen.*

A Vision of Satan in Panic

During a recent prayer time, God asked me if I would like to be shown what satan was doing. I politely declined, but God laughed, insisting that, "I want you to see this." From a distance, God allowed me to see into the workspace of satan. (Please know that this is not normal for me. Most of what I see is in God's heaven—*"things above"*—or in the earth realm).

As my eyes focused on the vision, I could sense the panic in the atmosphere around the evil one, and he was pacing up and down. Cast aside on the floor was a mangled white sheet attached to a stick—a rudimentary white flag of surrender. And God showed me satan's history with this white flag. Satan had made it some decades ago when the prayers and actions of the saints had been particularly strong at the end of the Second World War, when the Nazis were defeated and the Jewish people liberated.

However, satan had never actually used the flag and he hated that he had even made it, because in him is no thought of asking for clemency. But there *had* been a day when he was hard-pressed on every side and confusion had reigned in him. I watched him, when battles had not gone his way, pull out the white flag and then throw it back down again, manically angry that he had thought such a weak thought of quitting. Over time, that flag of surrender has been up and down, on and off the ground many times. I could see that it was screwed up and trampled on. This is another sign to us of the devil's weakness and his holding it should be an indication that there have been many situations in history when he did not win.

And now, as I looked on, satan was eyeing up his white flag again. His gaze moved between it and the calendar on his wall. He had seen what God had done to release power to the saints at the start of 2020 and he knew that he was in a weakened state and that his attacks were not going to be able to withstand what is being established against him in this hour.

Let's make this personal. There are some things in *your* life that are causing satan to cast his eye over to the white flag. There are situations where you have worn out the enemy and he is about to back off. You are mighty in Jesus and you have resisted, so take hope, he's about to flee!

Contrary to what the world is screaming right now, satan is *not* in the ascendancy. Satan has a headache that God has begun a new epoch of time. Choose not to give Satan any more credibility.

Contrary to what the world is screaming right now, satan is not in the ascendancy.

Note

1. *Helps Word-studies*, s.v. "Hades," Helps Ministries Inc., 1987, 2011 at www.thediscoverybible.com.

Chapter 2

Joy and Peace, Not Fear and Grief

The Atmosphere of Heaven

*For the kingdom of God is not a matter of eating
and drinking, but of righteousness, peace and joy
in the Holy Spirit* (Romans 14:17).

The Kingdom of God is righteousness, peace, and
joy, meaning that the atmosphere of Heaven is infused
with contentment and ease, with laughter and safety.
Heaven has no tension; it does not have stress; it is not
shaken. There is never a day when any inhabitant of
Heaven wakes up grumpy, angry, fearful, or anxious.
The atmosphere of Heaven is so wholesome and secure
that no one feels invisible or jealous. It is almost impos-
sible for us to truly comprehend what it must be like
to sit in that atmosphere of no decay, where nothing
negative could invade our emotions or our thinking or
infect and pollute our sense of wellbeing.

The absolutely amazing truth of Isaiah 65 is that when the new heavens and the new earth are created, the things of our past will be forgotten:

> *See, I will create new heavens and a new earth.*
> *The former things will not be remembered, nor*
> *will they come to mind* (Isaiah 65:17).

There will be no ability under any circumstances to recall what we consider to be "normal" emotional undulation here on this fallen earth. You will not be able to source emotional pain. You will never "walk" with a "limp" in your heart. You will not weep, you will not grieve, and you will not have a memory of the times when you did. In Heaven there will never be a child who only lives a few days or an old man who does not live out his years.

I do not want us to think, however, that we must endure torturous emotions on the earth, just hanging on by our fingernails until we can sit in pure, unadulterated righteousness, peace, and joy in our *future* home! We can experience it here and now. When we cry the prayer of Jesus that His Kingdom would come, *"on earth as it is in heaven"* (Matt. 6:10), we are contending for the atmosphere of peace, ease, security, and certainty to be established daily, here on earth, all around us.

God Laughs

I have watched God in Heaven laugh uproariously, dance furiously, and sing loudly. He is totally at ease. God laughs in Scripture, but His laughter is not reserved only for those comically funny moments. In fact, He uses laughter often in the Psalms when nations are in rebellion, partnering with idolatry, and outworking injustices. His laughter is not sarcastic, acerbic, or mocking. Rather, it is a sign of His unshakable Kingdom. He is so certain about the future that nothing can rob the ease and joy that He feels. When He tells us that His Kingdom is "joy," and when He asks us to pray for it to come, it's another way of saying that even in the midst of trial and in the darkest valley we can have an emotional response of ease and contentment that owns us—because our hope is in Him.

Even in the darkest valley, we can have an emotional ease and

**contentment—because our hope is
in Him.**

When laughter is first recorded in Scripture, it is in the story of Abraham and Sarah. In the midst of the excruciating pain and trauma of barrenness, we find that both Abraham and Sarah laugh. Laughter is the external sound of a heart that is nestled in security over the future; thus, the virtuous woman in Proverbs laughs without fear of the future:

> *She is clothed with strength and dignity,
> and she laughs without fear of the future*
> (Proverbs 31:25 NLT).

When we initially come to Jesus, a range of emotions determine our decision-making to choose Christ. Our hearts become convicted, the guilt and shame become too much to bear, and we have an expectation of an emotional change coming through our uniting ourselves with Jesus.

In the Psalms, King David identifies an emotion that is linked to our salvation when he sings, *"Restore to me the joy of your salvation*" (Ps. 51:12). Salvation is supposed to feel like something. It is supposed to have an associated emotion—the emotion of *joy*. This is the emotion of our salvation that, when fully working in us, makes us strong. *"The joy of the Lord is your strength"* (Neh. 8:10) is an oft-spoken truth, but we rarely understand how to apply it. Our tendency to independence leaves us short of biblical "normality." In error, we believe that our own determination makes us strong or that the force of our personality is our strength. Or perhaps we tell ourselves, "If I just keep my head down I'll get through this." But in the place of trials and tribulations, the medicine of Scripture is that I should seek the emotional *joy* of salvation to help me overcome. This does sound slightly foolish—after all, how can we be joyful and laughing when we're in the place of frustration? It's hard to laugh when you're terrified. But God provokes laughter as a sign that He has overturned the hierarchies of the world. (Jesus often interrupted the "normal" order of things. Even His birth was a transgression of normal order; He was rude at dinner parties; He spoke in parables; He was angry in temples; once He even called His favorite disciple,

"Satan"!) In this upside-down Kingdom of God, laughter and peace are the gifts given in our most unlikely situations. They are gifts, not always to change the circumstances *around* us, but to put a security *in* us about our future.

> **God provokes laughter as a sign that He has overturned the hierarchies of the world.**

We Are at War to Steward Joy and Peace

The kingdom of satan wants to slime you with grief, fear, sadness, and anxiety, the opposites of joy and peace. Therefore, for us as believers it is not business as usual. We are in a war to steward joy and peace and to stamp out our grief and fear.

I do believe that the Lord has navigated His church and His people to a place where they now stand at the door to their future. Now the pressure is on to navigate this tight space and to win with our daily issues so that we can steward life for many people in the days ahead. You are being reset and moved to enter a new era because God needs you in the right place for what is ahead.

God needs you in the right place for what is ahead.

What this means is that Father God is asking you to face some long-standing issues. Right now, God is forcing issues in you to the surface. Because of this you will feel pressure, you will feel that you're in a tight space, you will feel uncomfortable, you will feel the need to move, and you will feel the need to work with God's Spirit afresh, which is going to secure the major changes your life needs.

The Lord is saying to you today, "My hand is at your back and you will feel My pushing you forward. I have even used others around you to behave in ways that look unfair and they may even have been unkind to you. All that is happening around you is to ensure that you are shifting. Do not partner with offense. See, I am enabling you to be provoked to move in *My* time, and to walk out a new level of wholeness and freedom."

The earth is groaning for you to get into the right place. Can you even hear the sound of the earth longing for you to find and shift to the right place, for you to be revealed in your healed and fully well form? It's a time to decree that, "I am moving to the right place! I am moving to the place of wholeness, and I will be used by God." This is a day of your liberation.

Activation Prayer

Prayer walk around your home. Lay your hands on every window and door, commanding the atmosphere of Heaven to come.

Invite the Holy Spirit to infuse each room with righteousness, peace, and joy. Command all atmospheres that do not line up with the Kingdom of God to be removed immediately, in the name of Jesus Christ.

Speak over the atmosphere of your home that, "As it is in Heaven, so it will be here in my home!" Enjoy the process of sensing and seeing radical atmosphere changes that will impact your entire household—even those who are not yet believers.

Pray out loud:

> *Lord Jesus, would You restore to me the emotion of my salvation? I want to connect with the feelings of joy, contentment, and ease that You want to give me. My desire is to live in the atmosphere of Heaven every day. I banish emotional numbness from my life and I release my heart to feel the wonder of belonging to You, Jesus.*
>
> *In Your holy name, amen!*

Dealing with Fear

Have you ever thought that Adam and Eve must have had it easy in Eden? Were they lying back on sun-loungers, soaking up the sun while sipping drinks brought them on the backs of unicorns? Were they lazing around with nothing to do while angels massaged their feet?

This notion of a work-free "paradise" is of course all wrong. Adam and Eve had been given a massive mandate by God: they were to forge ahead into the world and to have dominion over it; they had fallen-angel enemies whom they were to be put under their feet; and, like God, they worked and then rested on the seventh day. They were in a battle, their days were numbered, and they were to tell a story with their lives—a story of overcoming, a story of struggle, a story of mortality woven together with victory.

In the rain and in the sun, in the snow and in the falling leaves, each moment was to count. The first man and woman were not to be lost in self-absorption but instead were to be focused on improving the earth. We, living thousands of years later, steward the same mandate: to face trouble and to scale it, to cast mountains into the sea, to be as bold as to even die for others, and every day to *choose well*. To live, all the while knowing that we cannot store up our breaths or somehow stop our heart beating and then restart it when the world is easier.

The average life expectancy is about seventy-five years old. Each of us therefore have a finite number of conscious hours remaining where we can focus on our own vanity or drag our feet about something.

I can partner with fear or I can speak so much courage over my own being that I'm a warrior who knows what it is to build the Kingdom of God. Whatever we choose, the endpoint is the same—we come to death. So, will we choose to live life to the full? Will we challenge ourselves to face our fears and to do things in spite of opposition? How fast can you run at life? How much *thankfulness* can you show? How deeply can you laugh—and can you *die by living well*?

I have long been taken by the author N.D. Wilson's story of the final hours of his grandfather's life.[1] Rather than focus on his own mortality, the old man chose passages of Scripture to write out for each of his children, their spouses, and their grandchildren—a total of forty-six people. Wilson recounts that, to the youngest of all, a two-month-old grandson, he handwrote a short message beside a Scripture verse:

> You may not remember me. I remember you and prayed for you when you were one day old. Great Grandpa.

That grandfather's determination to live well is summed up in those two simple sentences. Even when facing death, he was spending his life on blessing others. I told my own mum of this story when she was dying in a cancer hospice; she had bought Bibles for all her grandchildren (my children) and had already written a personal message in the front cover of each copy. Ever since, my children have dined on her words that urge boldness, confidence, and a passion for truth.

So to you, dear readers, the question is posed: Will you let fear rule, or will you determine that it has no hold on you?

Will you let fear rule, or will you determine that it has no hold on you?

How much fear do you have in your life?

Take a moment to consider this question carefully and then score yourself out of one hundred.

Now, ask the Holy Spirit if you got the percentage right! How does *He* score you? Are you fear-filled or are you fear-free?

Fear is an insulator. It does not easily allow you to move forward. It blocks your progress. Fear is a paralysis that locks up your decision-making abilities. Fear is a cancer to your emotional wellbeing. Fear hinders adventure and it lies to you about the reality of life in Christ. Fear will keep you out of time with the purposes of God. Fear is the daily drip, drip, drip of smallness that shrinks your world.

> ### Fear will keep you out of time with the purposes of God.

There is a tendency when living a life with fear to try to preserve and to protect what has gone before. Where you have had success in the past and where you might even have become established and well-regarded in your areas of expertise, walls get put up to defend what is yours and protect where you have arrived at. We fearfully protect the small and so we miss out on the huge adventuring moments of the future.

Trusting God Is a Process

Trusting God is a process; it's a lifestyle. It's not a one-time event in your history. Sometimes God plunges you into repeated daily, hourly, or even minute-by-minute moments when you don't know what you are doing and you cannot source the answer. Sometimes He shakes even the successes that He once blessed and enabled you to have, because fear has inoculated you and kept you out of the new thing and the new experiences that He has in store for you.

> **Sometimes God shakes even the successes that He enabled you to have, because fear has kept you out of the new things.**

Closing the Door to Fear

The story of Job in Scripture is challenging, largely because of the assertion he makes that:

> *What I feared has come upon me; what I dreaded has happened to me* (Job 3:25).

In essence, Job unconsciously chose how he would be shaken *by having a door of fear open in his life*. Fearing empowers the enemy to enter your life. Fear is a sure way to squander your defenses and hand access over to the forces of darkness. I have watched people fear certain illnesses so ferociously that they became paralyzed with the fear of getting sick. Sadly, just like Job, what they feared came upon them and they became ill. Christian maturity is an ability to keep spiritual "short accounts."[2] When fear comes knocking, there must be an ability to turn to face it and land it a knockout punch! We should not only *take captive every thought* (2 Cor. 10:5), but we should aim to take captive every thought at speed so that an initial low-level fear does not fester and become a stronghold that we subsequently struggle to dislodge.

If you have wrestled for years, I release to you now, in the name of Jesus, an ability to have "short accounts" in the spirit realm. I loose to you a swift spiritual responsiveness so that you may be able to turn back any battle at the gate, before it sweeps over you. *Speak over yourself right now that you receive the ability for short accounts, in Jesus's name!*

Once fear seeps into our church world it prevents whole masses of people from moving forward. It partners with a religiosity that protects the *status quo* and makes the people risk-averse. As fear spreads, the organization puts the brakes on, slows pace, and goes heavy on rules in an attempt to keep us all "inoffensive" to others. I believe that one of the best signs of high faith in a church is when that church *stops* something—when it is brave enough to end a program rather than just maintain the *status quo*. Faith gives leaders and their people the courage to kill what is not bearing fruit and even stops some things that may be productive but are "old wine." When did your church last stop something? The ability to bring an end to tasks and activities is a sure sign that you are winning against fear.

The ability to bring an end to tasks and activities is a sure sign that you are winning against fear.

This principle applies in the business marketplace as much as in the church world. I hear the Spirit of the Lord say, "Some have had business success, but it is time to stop selling some products so that others can come forth. It is time to stop some research so that the new can come to you. It is time to stop some connections so that the new can be held. It is time to stop living in some places so that the new can be occupied."

It is time to move from a *preservation* mindset to a *discovery* mindset. It is time to move from *fear* to *investment in the future*. It is time to move from being a *consumer* to becoming a *contributor*.

And God is speaking hope into our situations. I hear Him say, "I will help you deal with your history that has put you into protectionism mode and has robbed your discovery spirit. Begin to do what you are not sure you have the skill set for, even that which you feel unprepared for! Start the project—even if you are not sure it will work out, for I will back your small, adventuring steps," says the Lord.

Some of you who are meant to be pioneers have convinced yourselves that you are settlers and, especially as you have aged, there has been a settling. You are still growing up into the shape God has called you to be.

Activation Prayer

Again, this is best spoken out loud:

I trust You, God. (Let your heart hear these words of dependency and feel whole.) I trust You, God. I trust You, God, with my future. I trust You, God, with my health. I trust You, God, with my finances. I trust You, God, as the restorer of my relationships. I trust You, God, and the plans You have for my life.

Father, I lay down my preservation mindset and I pick up a discovery mindset. I lay down the paralysis of fear and I pick up an adventuring ability.

In Jesus's name, amen!

Notes

1. N.D. Wilson, *Death by Living* (Nashville: Thomas Wilson, 2013), 116-117.
2. "Short accounts" is a phrase that the Puritans used to say, as in, "to keep short accounts with God and men." In finance, it's the practice of paying off what you owe as soon as possible (a short account) rather than over an extended period of time (a long account).

Chapter 3

The Mindset of Deliverance

The issues of fear, sadness, anxiety, and grief are not only *emotions* that we wrestle with. They are also, on occasion, *in-dwelling demons*. Our freedom does not only come from positive-thinking and "pep-talking" ourselves, nor only from the good intention to grow character. Our freedom also comes in the casting out of demons. I love inner healing and honor the important place that inner healing tools and programs have in pastoring our Christian communities. However, if you do not cast out any associated demons along with inner healing, you will leave people only half restored.

Every place in our life where we have emotional damage and inner pain we have a potential foothold for a demonic stronghold to develop. Sometimes we partner with darkness completely inadvertently, but when we have a hole in our "hedge of protection" (see Job

1:10) because of unresolved pain, the enemy will try to gain access to further torment us.

> **Every place in our life where we have
> emotional damage and inner pain
> we have a potential foothold for a
> demonic stronghold to develop.**

At the end of this chapter there will be activation prayers to help you get fully free. But first, let's again dive into Scripture and look at the place of deliverance in the Kingdom of God. We'll do this so that we can answer important questions like, "Can a Christian have a demon?" and, "How do I stay safe when casting one out?"

Deliverance: An Integral Part of the Kingdom of God

And these signs will accompany those who believe: In my name they will drive out demons; they will speak in new tongues; they will pick up snakes with their hands; and when they drink deadly poison, it will not hurt them at all; they will place their hands on sick people, and they will get well (Mark 16:17-18).

This list of the signs that are demonstrated in the lives of those who believe in Jesus is unusual. If you and I were attempting to compile a list of what we should look for in a Christian's life, we would probably write something very different. Perhaps our list would read, *"And these signs will accompany those who believe: They will love each other; they will heal the sick, and they will be really great to spend time with!"* And yet, Scripture normalizes deliverance ministry as a sign that people should see demonstrated in your life as a believer. In fact, driving out or casting out demons is the first sign that the Kingdom of God is here—indicating that it should be our regular reality.

Jesus pushes the point even further in the gospel of Luke:

But if I drive out demons by the finger of God, then the kingdom of God has come upon you (Luke 11:20).

The way the Kingdom of God comes is by the *driving out of demons*. If you want to drop someone into a Kingdom culture—in other words, if you want Heaven to come on earth—then cast out their demons! And, according to Jesus, it's so straightforward for you that you'll be able to do it with your finger!

> *I have given you authority to trample on snakes and scorpions and to overcome all the power of the enemy; nothing will harm you* (Luke 10:19).

Again, this Scripture is challenging the people of God to not be backward and hesitant in facing demons. Jesus asks us today, just like He did of the disciples, "Who do you say that I am? If I am the all-powerful God and I have given you My authority, then truly nothing can harm you." You have been so blessed and such greatness sits on you because of Jesus Christ, *you* can deal with *all* the powers of the enemy!

If you want Heaven to come on earth—then cast out their demons!

These truths are challenging to many of us. We live with a prevailing Western ("Enlightenment") world-view. In other words, our thinking is supported by a surrounding scaffolding that is deeply unhelpful and frankly unbiblical when it comes to deliverance issues.

The lie of the Western worldview is that every effect has a physical cause; if you can't see it, touch it, taste it, smell it, or hear it, then it probably doesn't exist. It also trains us to think that all phenomena can, or eventually will, be explained or accounted for scientifically and that our reality is primarily material and mechanical. If there is a spiritual realm, the Western worldview says, it has absolutely no relation to, interaction with, or impact upon the physical realm.

However, the biblical worldview outlines clearly that physical and natural phenomena are put together by, and under, God. Angels do His bidding and demons (fallen angels) actively and energetically oppose His Kingdom. Miracles, medically unexplainable physical healings, the gifts of the Holy Spirit, and deliverance ministry are essential elements of a biblically real Christian life.

Freedom in Our Inner World

When we come to Jesus and seek Him as our Savior, the New Testament Greek word to describe our "salvation" is the noun *sótéria*. This word does not just mean, "I am saved." It is much more loaded than that. The fullness of *sótéria* encompasses the ideas of deliverance, salvation, welfare, prosperity, preservation, and safety.

Similarly, the Greek verb for "to save" in the New Testament is *sozo*, meaning to save, heal, preserve, and rescue—to deliver out of danger and into safety.

What we can see from these two words is that the biblical essence of being saved or inheriting salvation is that I am saved, healed, and *delivered*. It's a far-reaching package that does not only touch my eternal security but also ensures my day-to-day wellbeing by the removing of demonic oppression and the healing of diseases.

Furthermore, it is not accurate to say that one day in my *past only* I was saved, healed, and delivered. Neither is it the full picture to say that there will be a day in my *future* when I'm saved, healed, and delivered. More accurately, I am commanded by Jesus to walk out my salvation with fear and trembling as a daily lifestyle. Being saved is an ongoing reality.

Every day I engage with being saved, healed, and delivered!

Being saved is an ongoing reality.
Every day I engage with being saved,
healed, and delivered!

This truth should continually shape how we pray. When I repent, I acknowledge that I need a Savior, but I must not leave out the requirement for healing and deliverance too. Therefore, after repentance I break agreement with my emotional transgressions so that I can be healed. And I rebuke or cast out of me any demonic partnership I have formed so that I can be delivered. This means that any time spent with Jesus to fully work out your salvation means that you are repenting, renouncing, breaking agreement, and casting out demons as part of the regular "full-package deal" that Jesus bought for you and gave to you when you put your trust in Him as your Savior.

There is so much fear and suspicion around the demonic that we may have lost our perspective on how small a demon actually is, how easily removed it is—and how easily and frequently this should be happening in our lives.

Can a Christian Have a Demon?

I'm regularly asked the question of whether a Christian can actually "have" a demon. The quick and simple answer is "yes," but in order to more helpfully comprehend why this is, we must really be sure in our understanding of what happens to us at the point of our salvation. The Bible is very clear that when we come to Jesus we become one with Him in spirit, as Paul writes, *"But whoever is united with the Lord is one with him in spirit"* (1 Cor. 6:17).

At the very point of your conversion, the Holy Spirit took up residence inside you, whether you felt it or not, and you became *one in spirit with God*. That's remarkable! You and God are one in spirit.

You and God are one in spirit.

Activation

Ask Jesus to show you your inner reality, to reveal to you the shapes and colors of how you and the Holy Spirit of God are fused and flow together, as one, inside you. Do a Holy Spirit "M.R.I. scan" or "x-ray," where you switch on your spiritual eyes and see your internal spiritual world.

Top tip: This should be an enriching and empowering activation where you become aware that you are not without God but that His Spirit is your ever-present, constant internal truth.

Maturity of the Faith

A moment ago, we established that you are one with God in spirit. Where is the Holy Spirit at your conversion? He is not in your flesh. Neither is He in your emotions, and He is not in your heart. He is initially only in your *spirit*. You can be a born-again believer and yet be completely barren because you do not know how to experience the Holy Spirit. You can be impotent as a believer because you do not have the Holy Spirit flowing through all that you are. You will have

Him locked up and restricted to your spirit only. God lives in your spirit but He wants to be active in your soul, flesh, heart, will, emotions, and mind.

When Paul prays for us in Ephesians 3:16-21, he reinforces this truth and asks the Lord to strengthen us through His spirit, who is in our inner being: *"I pray that out of his glorious riches he may strengthen you with power through his Spirit in your inner being"* (Eph. 3:16).

Paul asks the Holy Spirit to *explode* inside of us (where he lives in our spirit) and, in doing so, to then move beyond that central place in order to also *saturate* our emotions, our heart, our will, our flesh, and our mind so that we would be strong and filled with the *power* that comes from the treasures of Heaven!

Paul's desire is that all of you—your inner man (your inner being), your flesh, your emotions, your will, your heart, and your soul—is strengthened with power, the very power that raised Jesus Christ from the dead, and that this happens because the spirit that you are one with explodes inside you.

The point is that we have to let the Holy Spirit loose to explode through all of us so that He is no longer contained in our spirit alone. The Holy Spirit, who is God inside of you, makes it a priority that you experience Him in every part of you. He desires a shift in you from mere religious "knowledge" into *abundant, tangible fullness!*

Sometimes we feel spiritually schizophrenic. We can say accurately, "I have all of the love of God in me" because it's in the Spirit, who is indwelling. We can, at the same time say, "I feel I have none of the love of God in me" and also be accurate, because it has not yet reached my heart for me to feel this.

By now, we should be getting a better idea of what true Christian maturity should be. Maturity of the faith is not about somehow growing more and more serious until you iron out any sense of being in love and you lose all your fervency and passion. Instead, maturity is knowing the Holy Spirit so well and having Him so released in you that Christ is formed or dwells in your heart. This will result in you feeling *more* in love, not less!

In this true maturity, you *won't* become a cantankerous, stoic, ornery, emotionally dead old grump—but you *will* feel more alive than you did at the start of your faith. Even your flesh will feel more alive in Jesus!

> **We have to let the Holy Spirit loose to explode through all of us so that He is no longer contained in our spirit alone.**

Prayer

This is great to pray every day!

> *Holy Spirit, I let You loose on the inside of me! Holy Spirit, explode in me because I do not want You contained in my spirit alone. Holy Spirit, fill and overflow in me so that my flesh does not sin and carry anger, fear, anxiety, raw grief, addiction, and frustration. Overflow in me so that I'm saturated and can move in the power that changes all things.*
>
> *Holy Spirit, detonate in me!*

Holy Spirit, I don't want to contain and limit You. Would You burst out of my spirit and touch my heart, mind, will, emotions, and flesh? I want to know what it is like to have You in all parts of who I am.

I want to begin to fellowship with You more than I have ever done before. I want to experience all that You have for me. I am desperate to know more of You. Thank You, God, amen!

Where Do Demons Live on a Christian?

Now that we've got a better understanding of the spiritual dynamics going on within each of us, we're able to return to the question of demons and ask, in particular, where demons live on a person who is a Christian?

Demons live on the flesh, where space is given and where the Holy Spirit has not been granted access. It is possible for a Christian to yield control of their bodies to a demonic spirit in the same way that they yield to the power of sin.

It is possible for a Christian to yield control of their bodies to a demonic spirit in the same way that they yield to the power of sin.

Can We Be Demon Possessed?

In short, no. The concept of demonic "possession" is not helpful—because it's not in the original Greek of the New Testament. Demon "possession" is not a biblical truth.

The term *demonic possession* was popularized by its appearance in the King James Version of the Bible but scholars all now agree that this is a poor translation of the word. It is biblically better—and more accurate—to use the word *demonized*.

Demon possession implies ownership and control but, of course, we are not owned by satan, nor are we controlled by satan. We belong to Jesus, and when it comes to "ownership," *"The earth is the Lord's, and everything in it"* (Ps. 24:1). So let's be clear: a Christian cannot be *demon possessed* because there is no such thing! A non-Christian cannot be *demon possessed* because there is no such thing. We can, however, be *demonized*, where we come under a high degree of influence from a demonic spirit.

The Mindset of a Deliverer

Almost everything we have done in church for decades has happened through the paradigm—the mindset—of the pastoral—the shepherd. We celebrate and honor our shepherd-pastors, but this default mindset is not the full picture and the only way of doing things. Shepherd-pastors taught us well that love should feel safe; that if we truly loved people there would be a tameness, cautiousness, and a conservativeness to our interactions. Highly prized in this paradigm was discretion, prudence, and always being on the safe side of decisions. In short, this has made us unadventurous and wary.

In C.S. Lewis's *The Lion, the Witch and the Wardrobe*, we read Mr. Beaver describe Aslan (an allegory of Jesus) to the children:

> "Aslan is a lion—the Lion, the great Lion." "Ooh," said Susan. "I'd thought he was a man. Is he…quite safe? I shall feel rather nervous about meeting a

lion." "Safe?" said Mr. Beaver. "Who said anything about safe? 'Course he isn't safe. But he's good. He's the King, I tell you."[1]

The whole message of the Bible is of a love that *fights* to deliver us—a love that is risky, unrelenting, unyielding and unabated. Apostles and prophets move in a paradigm that contains major elements of high risk. The love of the prophet, the love of the apostle, and the love of a deliverance minister is a *risky, bold love*. Our love for each other must have the lens of cautiousness ripped off it and we must see each other as worth getting free. Of course, we must also see ourselves as worth getting free! We must think about our friends, "I will take a bold step into your world, that I might value you and fight for your freedom—and also look at my own life, and value my own freedom."

A deliverance mindset never lets you stay as you are but instead gives extreme prominence to getting totally liberated from darkness. Now is the time to be infused with the mindset of determination that freedom matters and that deliverance is *every day*. Your freedom is worth pursuing! You are valuable, and Jesus wants you to be completely free.

**A deliverance mindset never lets
you stay as you are but instead gives
extreme prominence to getting totally
liberated from darkness.**

Activation Prayer

Physically put your hands on your head and pray for a realigning for your brain to think like a deliverance minister would:

> *Lord Jesus, I am sorry for where I have not valued freedom.*
>
> *Lord, would You place in me a new mindset— the thinking and abilities of a deliverer.*
>
> *I want to be just like You Jesus, whose aim was the deliverance of all humanity.*
>
> *In the name of Jesus, amen!*

Note

1. C.S. Lewis, *The Lion, The Witch and The Wardrobe* (Oxford: HarperCollins Publishers, 2005).

Chapter 4

The Business of Deliverance

In the midst of the coronavirus pandemic, you can feel the fear and sadness attempting to "slime" the people of God. Much of the fear has been long-resident in hearts and minds, but this current catastrophe has added, and provoked, fear to surface. We are not just dealing with the fear of this moment in time, but now we will focus on complete freedom from lifestyles of fear and grief. This means that you will need to look over your shoulder and into your history and cite moments when fear sowed seeds.

I am not aiming to secure simply a temporary sense of "wellbeing" by being able to prophesy around a moment in time. Rather, I am securing your long-term future with a more comprehensive freedom from fear approach. As you now begin the business of removing the demonic from your life, you will be able to steward peace, ease, contentment, and joy as a lifestyle in each and every subsequent moment of testing and shaking that may come your way.

Identifying Fear and Grief

It's time to start identifying whether you are carrying fear and grief. Take time to prayerfully consider the following list and mark any of the issues that you think you have active in your life, either in embryonic form or as highly established and dominant problems.

Spirits that operate under grief, depression, and fatigue:

- Despair
- Discouragement
- Despondency
- Defeatism
- Dejection
- Suicide
- Hopelessness
- Desire to die
- False guilt
- Insomnia
- Nightmares
- Feeling burdened
- Often disgusted with yourself
- Raw mourning
- Stuck in grief
- Sorrow
- Fatigue
- Tiredness

- Overtired
- Constant drowsiness
- Shutdown emotionally
- Weariness
- Laziness

- Sorrow
- Heartache
- Heartbreak
- Excessive crying
- Sadness
- Rawness

Some of these are natural and perfectly normal in the process of, for example, outworking and processing the death of a loved one. They only become a demonic consideration when you are stuck in them or they are overwhelming and outside of normal patterns and processes.

Spirits that operate under fear, anxiety, and hopelessness:

- Uneasiness
- Intense fear
- Stress
- Perpetual tension
- Palpitations

- Stabbing pains
- Hyperventilation
- Headaches
- Spasms in the neck

- Back pains
- Inability to relax
- Restlessness
- A sense of tiredness
- Dryness of mouth
- Diarrhea
- Nausea
- Changes in appetite
- Vomiting
- Frightening dreams
- Sweating
- Dizziness
- Light headedness
- Irritability
- Depression
- Hypochondria
- Mental illness

- Panic disorder
- Dependence on others
- Paranoia
- Anxiety neurosis
- Phobias
- Irrational fears
- Fear of losing control
- Fear of going mad
- Emotional stress
- Psychosexual disorder
- Tremor of the hands
- A sense of impending doom
- Tension of the muscles
- Difficulty swallowing

- Post-Traumatic Stress Disorder (PTSD)
- Fear of losing loved objects
- Fear of having a chronic illness
- Fear of the future
- Fear of failure
- Obsessive Compulsive Behavior (or OCD)
- Tendency to sigh or over-breathe
- Severe pain
- Mimicking serious illness
- Constant need to urinate or defecate
- Fear for the safety of family and friends
- De-personalization—the sense of being cut off from yourself
- De-realization—the sense of being cut off from reality/the world
- A raised level of arousal in your central nervous system
- The constant feeling that something bad is going to happen
- Difficulty getting to sleep / constantly waking / unable to get back to sleep
- Confusion
- Nightmares

- Anxiety
- Worry
- Inferiority complex
- Feeling rejection
- The need to be in control
- Feeling torment
- Feeling dread
- Fear of death
- Terror
- Over-carefulness/caution
- Guilt
- Fear of man
- Nervous disorders
- Fear of God (an unrighteous fear)
- Fear of hell
- Fear of judgment
- Paranoia

- Fear of poverty
- Fear of people
- Panic
- Fright
- Unbelief
- Timidity
- Faithlessness
- Alarm
- Uncourageous
- Unholy dread
- Dismay
- Spirit of the coward
- Fear and trembling
- Nervousness
- Shock
- Trauma
- Loss of courage
- Panic

- Doubt
- Paralyzing fear
- Fear that causes fainting
- Fear that causing heart issues/ attacks

- Suicide
- Death
- Insomnia
- Morbidity
- Despondency

Chapter 5

Top Tips for Removing Your Demons

Before we move on to the prayers and actions that will lift these demonic things off your life, let's get practical about the "mechanics" of removing them. In other words, what do we need to know and what do we need to do to shift these issues of our life?

1. Binding

In fact, no one can enter a strong man's house without first tying him up [binding him]. Then he can plunder the strong man's house (Mark 3:27).

You cannot get free without first binding the strongman. Binding is a priority. Speak over yourself: "I bind any and all strong men demons operating in my life." This puts you biblically in the right place to proceed with your freedom.

You cannot loose before you have bound; you cannot put in a prison that which you have not yet arrested. You cannot have freedom before tying up the spirit. Once they are bound then it's time to set the battle lines.

2.   Set the Agenda

Sometimes demons fight back because they have never been challenged. They are not used to working with empowered Christians and have not often been commanded before! Therefore, speak over yourself: "Demons! You will be leaving today!" Then give them the order for how it will be done: "You will do no harm; you will not make a fuss; you will not fight back; you will leave cleanly and completely, in Jesus's name." You decide how this goes; you set the tone and you determine the parameters of demonic behavior.

3.   No More Petition Prayers!

Getting free is a warfare situation. You are not coaxing, cajoling or begging demons. You are forcefully decreeing in the name and authority of Jesus! Never get into a back-and-forth conversation. Always remain in a warfare mindset, certain of your authority, knowing that when you resist the demonic they must flee (see James 4:7).

4.   Out on the Breath

A demon is a spirit—it is breath; it is wind or air. This is one of the most important things that you need to know: *demons come out on the breath*. Therefore, take big, deep breaths and blow them out—or cough, burp, or yawn. When keeping spiritual "short accounts" in our family we simply repent, break agreement with any demons or issues, and then we calmly blow out gently, on the breath, all oppression.

5.   Burn with Holy Fire

Demons hate the purifying fire of God! Therefore, as part of your times with Jesus, ask Him to burn you with holy fire and this will quickly assist your liberation.

6.   Find a Friend

It is always best practice to minister freedom with a good friend present. Sometimes when dealing with our own blind spots we need an intervention from kindly, godly warriors. The issues that daily require "short accounts" are easy to do by yourself. However, if you know that you have some very significant long-standing fear, anxiety, or grief issues, please make sure that you have somebody on the end of a phone or, even better, in the room as you pray the prayers that will follow.

7. Re-Fill the Space

> *When an impure spirit comes out of a person, it goes through arid places seeking rest and does not find it. Then it says, "I will return to the house I left." When it arrives, it finds the house unoccupied, swept clean and put in order. Then it goes and takes with it seven other spirits more wicked than itself, and they go in and live there. And the final condition of that person is worse than the first* (Matthew 12:43-45).

Demons co-operate with each other. They will go and seek seven stronger demons to re-inhabit the place that they have just left if we do not first re-fill this space. In fact, you can actually make yourself *worse*, if you do not want to be well and you do not want the

Holy Spirit to reside in the place where the demons have sat. This is why *we do not do* deliverance ministry on non-Christians (unless it is part of their salvation experience), because the Holy Spirit must inhabit the space vacated by the demonic. So, as you get free, remember to continually invite the Holy Spirit to flood all of your life.

Chapter 6

Our Open Doors and the Prayers to Shut Them

Like a fluttering sparrow or a darting swallow, an undeserved curse does not come to rest (Proverbs 26:2).

I am not "fair game" for the enemy! He *cannot* do whatever he likes in my life. Proverbs 26 is like warming comfort for our hearts—undeserved curses cannot land on us or negatively affect us. Therefore, if *we* do have some demonic interference, the first question must always be, "Where is my open door?"

We will now examine four of the ways that we can "open doors," put "holes in our hedges," or become "deserving" of curses—and we'll pray into each area.

Open Door One

Generational Issues

Have you ever noticed that the children of addicts often become addicts themselves, or that the anger that manifests in your life was also present in one of your parents? The Bible is clear in outlining generational curses that visit family lines, some even up to ten generations. Some of the issues that you battle and that you marked in Chapter 4 you will see not just as your own issues but as *inherited* battle grounds.

I remember a client who labored under a family sexual curse and was struggling with lesbianism. She endured years of emotional torture as she battled with her sexuality, but as soon as the family curse was broken she was completely healed and set free from all sexual perversions!

Pause—Action

Ask the question: Have I inherited something that needs to be cut off? Is there something that I constantly battle against that has been passed down to me?

If so, pray these prayers out loud:

In the name of Jesus Christ, I renounce, break, and loose myself from all demonic curses that came to me from my mother, father, grandparents, and generational line. I thank You, Lord, for setting me free.

In the name of Jesus Christ, I renounce, break, and loose myself and my family line from all powers, bondages, or bonds of physical or mental illness that have come upon me or my family line because of my parents' actions or the actions of my other ancestors.

In the name of Jesus Christ, I repent of all the sins of my mother and father and their mothers and fathers back ten generations, which allowed demonic spirits and curses to pass to me.

I specifically repent of the sins and iniquities that allowed the demon spirits of rejection, bitterness, depression, fear, guilt, grief, infirmities, and lust, and their nests or families, to pass to me when I was conceived. I renounce all those demons, and I break every curse that allows those spirits to remain within me. I renounce and break all resulting curses and connected spirits, and I cancel them in the name of Jesus. I ask You, God, to bless all my remaining family line.

God, I confess to You the sin of my parents, and I ask You to forgive them. I confess that my grandparents and great-grandparents sinned. I forgive them, and I ask You to forgive them. I also confess to You the financial sin of myself and my generations. I renounce it and ask You to forgive my financial sin and remove the resulting curses from me.

Open Door Two

Curses

Curses are spoken words to bring misfortune or evil into a life. It is easy to blame the witchcraft community for standing against us, but far more sinister is the self-cursing that we do. When you self-curse, you speak the words of satan and you give him high-level access to send a myriad of demons in to your life.

For example:

- I am not intelligent / pretty / gifted.

- I will always be financially struggling.

- I will never get a job.

- I will never get married.

- I will never get on top of my work load.

- I will never get promoted.

- I never hear from God.

- Life will always be like this.

- I will always be scared.

- I will always battle like this.

- This is just the way I am made.

The number of self-hating, self-loathing, spiritually limiting, and breakthrough-capping demons that have charged through the open doors of self-cursing is staggering! We need to stop serving satan's mission in our lives and instead believe the report of God about us. If satan has any access, it is because we gave it to him. Stop giving him access! We must get biblically balanced about demons. They do not have *carte blanche* to walk all over your life.

Pause—Action

Ask God to show you a curse that you have spoken over your life that has put a hole in your hedge.

If you have self-cursed, pray these prayers out loud:

In the name of Jesus Christ, I repent and ask forgiveness for every time that I have cursed myself or others in word or in prayer. I choose to break agreement with every self-cursing word, spoken and thought, and I choose to now bless those whom I have cursed.

List the names of those people you need to bless.

I renounce and revoke the curses I have spoken over my own life. I choose to receive blessing from You, Father God, and I now choose to think and speak well of myself as a child of God.

Open Door Three

Personal Partnership with Sin

God has given man the right to choose his lifestyle. In our sin we open the door to the demonic.

The following prayer is for personal repentance, to clean your slate with God, and to bind evil and free yourself from demonic influence.

Pause—Action

Pray out loud:

> *Jesus, I confess all my sins and repent. I ask You to forgive me and cleanse me in Your blood. I come to You as my Deliverer. I am sorry for each and every way, known and unknown, I have sinned against You. You know all my sins (name them), and all the things that bind, torment, defile, and harass me.*

I now loose myself from every dark spirit, evil influence, satanic bondage, and every spirit in me that is not the Spirit of God.

Open Door Four

Unforgiveness

Unforgiveness hinders the flow of God and His freedom in your life. It actually puts you in opposition to God. When you have limited God's movement in your life you have, in turn, empowered satan. I usually find that if a client has become stuck in a freedom session and the demon is resisting coming out, it is usually because there is an issue of unforgiveness somewhere. Even though people may feel that they have forgiven their parents, their partner, or their abuser (for example), there is often another, deeper level of forgiveness for them to delve into.

One of the most freeing things that we can do is to make ourselves say aloud, "I release forgiveness to… [name the person]." Even if you don't *feel* it in that moment, your heart will eventually catch up with your declaration.

Releasing forgiveness is not ever saying that the person who did you harm was right. Instead it is releasing pain from you. Sometimes you may have to do this for several days at a time. Ultimately, Jesus wants to take you to the place where you can pray blessing on those who have hurt you—this does take some courage.

Pause—Action

Ask God, "Is there anyone I need to release forgiveness to (or again)?"

> *Lord Jesus, I have a confession to make.*
>
> *I have not always loved but have resented certain people and have unforgiveness in my heart. I call upon You, Lord, to help me forgive them.*
>
> *It is my will and desire to forgive them from my heart. Take the unforgiving spirit away and take all the hurt and pain away.*
>
> *I now forgive (name each person, living and dead, who comes to mind), and I ask You to forgive them also, Lord.*

All four of these prayers have cleared the ground for the final task of commanding demons to go once and for all. You should be feeling lighter!

Stand Up and Decree Out Loud

> *Jesus, I come before Your throne and I use Your name, which is high above every other name. And, in the name of Jesus, I speak to all the demons that have tormented my life—those of fear, anxiety, and grief (also name the others from the list above) and say, "Today you are leaving my body. You are going to leave easily, cleanly, and on my breath, without doing me any harm. I do not give you permission to remain in me."*
>
> *I bind the strongman and limit any lashing out or pain that you would seek to inflict against me.*
>
> *I have destroyed the scaffolding that you have made in my life and I have destroyed the thrones that you sit on. In the name of*

*Jesus, you leave me now! I command You out
on my breath.*

Take a deep breath in, and then blow out. You may
need to do this a couple of times—but please don't
hyperventilate, there is no need!

*I burn you with the holy fire of God. I break
all agreement with you, and I decree over my
body that Jesus Christ is Lord of all that I am.
The fire of God now consumes your future
plans for me and incinerates the seeds you
have sown and any other demons you invited
into partnership with you. I declare myself
free because of the power of Jesus.*

As the demons come out on the breath, they can
sometimes get stuck in the throat as the last place they
touch before they leave. Sometimes it is helpful to arti-
ficially cough to remove the final remnant of darkness.

*In Jesus's name, I decree that I am rid of you
demonic inflictions and I decree that I am a*

demon-free zone. My grief is gone and my fear is gone!

I now receive the infilling of the Holy Spirit to sit in all the places that the powers of darkness operated within me.

Take some time to sit with your hands open and receive the infilling of the Spirit of God.

Well done, you are now free!

Chapter 7

What Now? After Care

It's important to share your journey with others, to debrief in trusted places, and to share the new spacious place that you find yourself in. This will help you settle into your new norm.

Often after such significant ministry, you can feel a little bit dizzy or light-headed as your physical frame readjusts to this new liberation. Be kind to yourself in the next few days—rest well and eat healthily, because you need to allow yourself to settle in this expanded place.

Driving out demons, you will have learned, is easy! However, habits take more time. Therefore, the days that follow the breathing out of demons require *intentionality*. Linger in your time with God, asking Him to show you what it is like to spend time without those longstanding issues present. The following post-freedom prayer is also very useful:

Father God, I rejoice in this new beginning of freedom in my life. Thank You for the awesome gift of being liberated by You. I embrace the work You are doing in me, and I accept all that You have for my life.

I choose to keep my eyes, vision, and focus on You, Lord Jesus. Help me to set my face like flint and to run the race You have set before me. I speak to my mind and my thoughts, and I tell them to stay focused on and captivated with the Lord. God, protect me, my mind, and my emotions from vain imaginations, lies of the enemy, and demonic strongholds. I choose to live a life founded on prayer, based on the Word of God, and saturated in worshiping, praising, and exalting You.

I love You, Lord. You are an awesome, magnificent, faithful, all-powerful, loving God. Fill me, Holy Spirit, with Your presence, and guide and direct me to lead a humble, teachable life of Kingdom integrity. And God, I ask for personal encounters with You. Jesus, I want to know You more. I ask that You show Yourself to me in ways that I have not known. I welcome You to speak to me and to show Yourself to me. I want to know You more.

Transform me, Lord. Amen!

Chapter 8

The Future: Setting the Tone in the Midst of Lockdown!

In the midst of the current coronavirus pandemic, it is not always helpful to ask questions like, "When will it end?" for this is our new *normal*—a world where everything familiar has fundamentally changed. It is better is to ask God to establish you in a new place and to keep you free to flourish in this new epoch.

In Genesis, the people of God were given a mandate to rule, reign, and have dominion in the earth realm. This was not for the church to be arrogant or heavy-handed, but rather to understand that we are weighty, trusted spiritual beings who can shadow atmospheres and shift them—because this is our God-given call.

We see a key progression of significant types of miracle building through the New Testament. It starts with the woman with the issue of blood clinging on to the hem of Jesus's garment (see Matt. 9:20). She has to reach out to touch one piece of cloth to be healed. The miracle grows, and the next time we see this sort of supernatural event is when Paul's handkerchiefs are sent out to the masses (see Acts 19:12). This time, it is not one piece of cloth—it's a multiplication, so that more can be impacted. Finally, we watch Peter, who now needs no cloth or garment—simply a shadow—to shift powers of darkness. His shadow heals the sick (see Acts 5:15). I believe that the progression of this in the lives of those who are called by Jesus to do "greater works" (see John 14:12) is that we now shadow atmospheres in our homes, neighborhoods, communities, cities, and nations.

What you choose, who you are, and the level of freedom that you steward—the amount of God's glory and fire that you emanate—will set the atmospheric tone for the wellbeing of your community, even those whom you do not know within it. *This* is why the management of your ongoing freedom matters!

**The level of freedom that you steward
will set the atmospheric tone for the
wellbeing of your community.**

The Lord began to speak to me about demonic cycles in nations that we are going to have to break for the wellbeing of many. God explained that every time the world or a nation had been shaken or had experienced a significant trauma (for example, war or famine), the enemy had then placed over that nation a demonic blanket of raw, debilitating grief.

The Lord said to me that fear was the beginning issue as crisis unfolded, but the long-term damage would be the weight of depression that would sit over millions of people. It is into this future that we must stand counter to the atmosphere of satan. We must know personally how to own joy for ourselves so that we can shadow nations back into stability, ease, and emotional contentment. Your freedom is not simply for your own enjoyment—*it is for the wellbeing of many.*

Power Back in Your Home

In the middle of our quarantining, social distancing, and isolation, the Lord is restoring the family unit and restoring homes as key places of spirituality. Do not waste this crisis, for God is putting His power back into your home and allowing His Spirit to be manifest there.

A Great Day for the Church

This is a great day for the church. Although it is hard to not see each other face to face, God has a purpose in the midst of our separation. Church had become more about the *structure* than the *presence* and was steeped in *overfamiliarity* rather than *reverential awe*. We were franchising what we had seen work elsewhere, without an authentic understanding of what our own remit was from God. In essence, we were more religious than relational, and we were blinded by this.

Through this time, God is going to put into our hearts a fresh yearning, not just for His courts, but also a yearning for one another. We will return to gathering with a reverential fear of the Lord that has been missing for a generation. This will enable the fire of God to fall in a way that we have been praying for, for years!

> **We will return to gathering with a reverential fear of the Lord that has been missing for a generation.**

Harvest, Awakening, and Deliverance

I have seen, flying around our earth, three angels. The first was the *Angel of the Harvest*—these are the days of us being provoked to cry for souls as the one billion soul harvest begins!

He is joined by the *Angel of Awakening*, where there is a great and extreme visitation of the Holy Spirit and revival coming to the earth.

The third angel is a deliverance angel, where we will know Jesus as the Deliverer—and we, in turn, will be known as "the Delivered" and those who can bring freedom.

The Gates of Hades Will Not Prevail!

Through the crisis and the trauma and our own personal battling, Christ Jesus is still building His church and the Gates of Hades will not prevail against it! These are the days of glory fire landing on us, when we will burn as flames and, in turn, set the world on fire! You were born for this epoch; steward your freedom so that you may not live like those to the left and the right of you but so that you may live with an abundant life so evident in you that you are chased and grabbed hold of by those who are seeking Jesus.

About Emma Stark

Emma Stark is an Irish prophet known around the world for her authority and authenticity. A fourth generation Bible teacher, she communicates with a rare clarity, humor, and Celtic boldness. Emma is a core leader of the British Isles Council of Prophets and, with her husband, leads Glasgow Prophetic Centre and the Global Prophetic Alliance. Every year thousands travel to their center in Scotland to hear from God, receive freedom, and be equipped as prophetic warriors.

Lightning Source UK Ltd.
Milton Keynes UK
UKHW022021250820
368801UK00012B/2839

9 780768 456790